Cheetahs

by Barbara Keevil Parker

Lerner Publications Company • Minneapolis

To Jon, Donna, Allie, Nicholas, Samantha. May you run swift as the cheetah.
—BKP

My thanks to Duane Parker, Pamela Parker Halverson, the Education Department staff at Roger Williams Park Zoo in Providence, Rhode Island, and my writers group for reviewing and commenting on this manuscript. I am grateful to Mary Winget, whose editorial expertise polished the text.

Photographs are reproduced with the permission of: © Michele Burgess, front cover, pp. 6, 8, 11, 13, 14, 15, 16, 17, 18, 19, 20, 21, 24, 25, 26, 27, 28, 29, 30, 31, 32, 33, 34, 35, 36, 37, 39, 40, 41, 42, 43; © Fritz Polking/Visuals Unlimited, pp. 4, 10, 22, 23, 46–47; © Leonard Rue III/Visuals Unlimited, p. 7; © Kevin Schafer, pp. 9, 12; © Staffan Widstrand/CORBIS, p. 38.

Lerner Publications Company
A division of Lerner Publishing Group
241 First Avenue North
Minneapolis, MN 55401 U.S.A.

Website address: www.lernerbooks.com

Library of Congress Cataloging-in-Publication Data

Parker, Barbara Keevil.
    Cheetahs / by Barbara Keevil Parker.
        p.   cm. — (Early bird nature books)
    Includes index.
    Contents: The world's fastest mammal—Home sweet home—
Hunting and eating—Cheetah cubs—Cheetahs in danger.
    ISBN: 0–8225–3053–8 (lib. bdg. : alk. paper)
    1. Cheetah—Juvenile literature. [1. Cheetah.] I. Title.
II. Series.
QL737.C23P354 2005
599.75'9—dc22   2003027287

Manufactured in the United States of America
1 2 3 4 5 6 – JR – 10 09 08 07 06 05

Contents

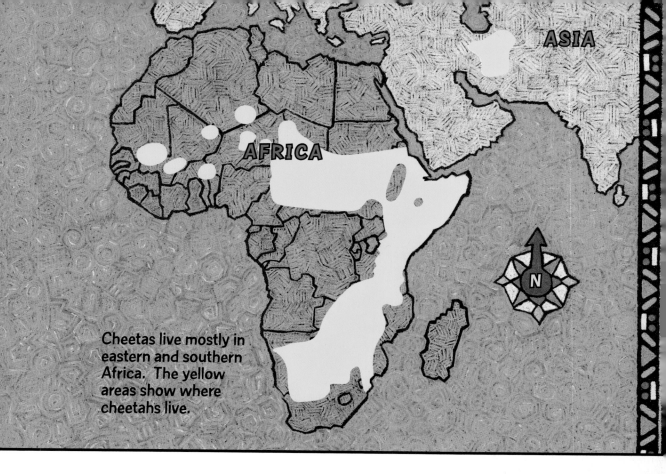

ASIA

AFRICA

N

Cheetas live mostly in eastern and southern Africa. The yellow areas show where cheetahs live.

Be a Word Detective

Can you find these words as you read about the cheetah's life? Be a detective and try to figure out what they mean. You can turn to the glossary on page 46 for help.

coalition
cubs
den
endangered
extinct

habitat
litter
mantle
poachers
predators

prey
savannas
territory

Chapter 1

The Cheetah's scientific name is Acinonyx jubatus. Cheetahs can see a long way on the open plains. What might this cheetah be watching?

The World's Fastest Land Animal

The dry grass stands still and deep on the open plains. Two golden eyes peer through the grass. They are the eyes of a cheetah. She watches a herd of gazelles.

One gazelle drifts away from the herd. The cheetah watches. Then she bursts from her hiding place and races toward the gazelle. Quick as the wind, the cheetah runs toward the gazelle.

A gazelle is a kind of antelope. This male Thomson's gazelle has wandered off from the herd to get a drink of water.

The gazelle darts away. The cheetah's claws grab the earth. Her tail swings through the air. She swats the gazelle with one of her powerful front paws. The gazelle loses its balance. It falls to the ground.

Cheetahs usually don't have to travel far to find an animal to hunt.

Cheetahs are fast from the moment they start to run.
They move forward like an arrow shot from a bow.

Cheetahs are the world's fastest runners. From standing still, they can reach 45 miles per hour in about two seconds. That's much faster than our fastest human runners. Humans can only run up to 27 miles an hour. At top speed, cheetahs can run 70 miles per hour. That is faster than cars on most highways.

But cheetahs can't run that fast for long. If they can't catch an animal quickly, they give up the hunt. Cheetahs run in giant bounds. They can cover about 20 feet with each leap. That's farther than the length of a small truck.

Every part of a cheetah's body is designed for speed.

A cheetah's back bends easily. This helps the cheetah to run fast.

What makes cheetahs such fast runners? Their bodies are slim. They have no extra weight to slow them down. Their backs are springy, like a Slinky toy. Their legs are long and strong. Cheetahs' claws work like cleats on sport shoes. They grip the ground.

11

Most cats have sharp claws. But a cheetah's claws are dull, like a dog's claws.

Cheetahs are part of the cat family. So are lions, tigers, leopards, and jaguars. Most cats can hide their claws inside their paws. A house cat pulls in its claws when it is resting. When it wants to scratch something, it pushes its claws out. But a cheetah can't hide its claws. A cheetah's claws are always out, ready for action.

A large male cheetah can weigh up to 120 pounds.

Cheetahs weigh about 100 pounds. It would take about 10 house cats to weigh as much as one cheetah. Including their tails, big cheetahs can be 7 feet long. That's as long as an adult's bicycle.

Cheetahs have long tails. The tails end with black rings and a white tip. Their long tails help them to balance.

Cheetahs have yellow or tan fur with black spots. The throat and belly are white with black spots. Each cheetah's spots are different. People who work with cheetahs look at their spots to tell them apart.

A cheetah's face has dark lines that are called tear lines. It almost looks like the cheetah is crying.

Chapter 2

A cheetah's colors help it hide in tall grass. What are grasslands in Africa called?

Home Sweet Home

Cheetahs live in eastern and southern Africa. They live in large grasslands called savannas.

Savannas are the cheetah's habitat. A habitat is the area where a kind of animal lives. A cheetah's habitat must have plenty of food and plenty of space. Africa's savannas have both food and space.

This cheetah is chasing a gazelle across a savanna.

Cheetahs can't roar like lions and tigers. Instead, they purr like house cats.

Cheetahs live alone or in small groups. Female cheetahs live alone in their habitat, except when they have babies.

This cheetah is standing on a tree branch to look around.

Some male cheetahs live in groups of two to four. These cheetahs are usually brothers. A group of male cheetahs is called a coalition.

Each coalition chooses its own place to live. That place is called a territory. A territory is like a human's yard and house. The coalition will chase other male cheetahs away from its territory.

Male cheetahs from the same family usually live together.

Chapter 3

This cheetah is eating an antelope. What are animals that hunt and eat other animals called?

Hunting and Eating

Cheetahs are predators (PREH-duh-turz). Predators are animals that hunt and eat other animals. Cheetahs hunt small or medium-sized animals, such as antelopes. The animals that cheetahs hunt are called their prey.

Many different kinds of antelopes live in eastern and southern Africa. Two kinds are impalas and gazelles. Gazelles are one of the cheetah's favorite prey.

Gazelles and impalas are two kinds of antelopes. They live on the dry, grassy plains of eastern and southern Africa.

Cheetahs are not picky eaters. When cheetahs can't find antelopes, they eat rabbits, ostriches and other birds, bird eggs, lizards, or frogs.

Most adult cheetahs eat every two to five days. But mother cheetahs with babies need to eat every day.

A cheetah flicks its tail to one side when it wants to turn.

It takes only seconds for a cheetah to outrun an impala.

Cheetahs are good hunters. They are not strong, like lions and tigers. So cheetahs use their speed to catch prey.

Cheetahs use a lot of energy when they run fast. They get tired after running only a short distance. Cheetahs must get close to their prey before they start to chase it. On half of their hunts, cheetahs do not even catch their prey.

This cheetah is watching for prey from high in a tree.

When a cheetah hunts, it looks for a herd of gazelles. When it sees a herd, the cheetah slowly walks toward the gazelles. Sometimes the cheetah hides in the tall grass so the gazelles can't see it. Then the cheetah waits and watches.

The cheetah picks one gazelle to chase. Then the cheetah springs forward and speeds toward its prey. The chase lasts only about 20 seconds. When the cheetah catches up to its prey, it hits the gazelle with its paw. The cheetah knocks the animal down. Then the cheetah bites the animal's throat so it can't breathe.

A cheetah bites down on the throat of a gazelle.

A cheetah stands over a gazelle it has killed. The cheetah needs to rest after hunting.

The cheetah does not eat right away. Instead, it drags the dead animal away. The cheetah takes its prey to a shady spot if it can find one.

Then the cheetah rests. It pants like a dog while it catches its breath. A cheetah may rest for 30 minutes before starting to eat.

After catching its breath, the hungry cheetah eats its meal.

When a cheetah finally does eat, it gulps its food. It easts fast so other animals can't steal its meal.

Cheetahs are not fighters. For this reason, other animals such as lions, leopards, and hyenas often steal a cheetah's food. Cheetahs might growl at animals that come near their food. But they usually give up their dinner without a fight.

Chapter 4

A mother cheetah stands guard over her babies. What are baby cheetahs called?

Cheetah Cubs

A female cheetah usually has two to four babies. But she may have up to eight babies at a time. Baby cheetahs are called cubs. A group of cheetah cubs that are born together is called a litter.

Cheetah cubs are born in a den. A den is a quiet, safe place. The den might be under thick bushes. Or it might be a quiet place behind some rocks.

A cheetah mother takes good care of her cubs. Baby cheetahs cuddle up to their mother while she rests.

Cubs can be born at any time of the year. Each cub weighs less than 1 pound. That's less than a pint of ice cream weighs. Just like kittens, cheetah cubs are born with their eyes closed. Cubs open their eyes for the first time 4 to 11 days after birth.

Raising cheetah cubs is hard work. Some cubs die from getting too much sun or from rain that makes them wet and cold.

Cheetah cubs drink their mother's milk until they are three to six months old.

A mother cheetah feeds her cubs and takes care of them. Their father does not help her. The cubs drink their mother's milk. They cuddle close to her body to keep warm.

At birth, cheetah cubs have short, dark fur with tiny spots. Soon a thick, gray coat, called a mantle, grows on their heads and down their backs. The fur of the mantle sticks up. It makes the cheetah cubs look bigger than they are. The mantle fur starts to fall out when the cubs are about three months old. Soon the young cheetahs look like adults.

Thick, long fur on the backs of cheetah cubs helps to protect them.

Cheetah cubs are playful. This one is playing with its mother's tail.

Cheetah cubs can walk when they are about 10 days old. They chirp to call for their mother. They sound like little birds. Their mother answers them with the same chirping sound.

Cheetah cubs follow their mother down a dirt road.

When the cubs are about six weeks old, they start to follow their mother when she hunts prey. The mother cheetah shares the prey with her babies. But the cubs still drink their mother's milk too.

When the cubs are about six months old, the mother cheetah teaches them to hunt. She brings them live prey so they can practice catching it. One-year-old cheetahs try to hunt by themselves. Three or four months later, they can hunt on their own.

A cheetah and her cubs chase each other. Cubs learn hunting skills as they play.

Chapter 5

This young cheetah is using a tree as a lookout. How many cheetahs are left in Africa?

Cheetahs in Danger

One hundred years ago, there were more than 100,000 cheetahs in Africa. But only about 12,000 are left. Why did so many cheetahs disappear?

Cheetahs are not dangerous to people. But people are the cheetahs' most dangerous enemy. Some people kill cheetahs for their beautiful spotted fur.

Most countries have laws against hunting cheetahs. But some hunters break the law and kill cheetahs. These hunters are called poachers. Other laws stop people from buying cheetah skins. But people still break the law by selling and buying skins.

Long ago, people kept cheetahs as pets. People also used cheetahs to hunt antelope and deer.

People are turning the grasslands into farms or towns. The prey animals have no place to live. They go to other places, or they die off. Cheetahs have less space to hunt and fewer prey animals to eat. Without prey to hunt, cheetahs starve.

Fences built to protect farm animals and crops cut up open areas that cheetahs need for hunting.

Some people are curious about cheetahs. Cheetahs are also curious about humans.

Many people take trips to see wild animals. Sometimes they scare away the animals. Prey running from people make it hard for cheetahs to catch prey.

Less than half of young cheetahs live to become adults. While the mother cheetah is hunting, predators such as lions and leopards may kill her cubs. Many cheetah cubs get sick and die. Some cheetahs starve. These problems have made cheetahs endangered. Endangered means that so few cheetahs are living that they might die out forever.

This cheetah is too thin. It has not had enough to eat.

People are trying to save cheetahs so they will not become extinct. If the cheetah becomes extinct, there will be none left in the world.

While mother cheetahs are hunting, lions may find and kill her cubs.

This cheetah lives at an African wildlife park.

Some Africans are capturing wild cheetahs. People move these captured cheetahs to wildlife parks. In the parks, wild animals are safe.

You may never see a cheetah on the African savannas. But you can still see cheetahs. Visit zoos and wildlife parks to watch and learn about cheetahs. If you see a cheetah run, you will believe it is the fastest animal on earth.

A mother cheetah and her cub sit on a small hill.

On Sharing a Book

As you know, adults greatly influence a child's attitude toward reading. When a child sees you read, or when you share a book with a child, you're sending a message that reading is important. Show the child that reading a book together is important to you. Find a comfortable, quiet place. Turn off the television and limit other distractions, such as telephone calls.

Be prepared to start slowly. Take turns reading parts of this book. Stop and talk about what you're reading. Talk about the photographs. You may find that much of the shared time is spent discussing just a few pages. This discussion time is valuable for both of you, so don't move through the book too quickly. If the child begins to lose interest, stop reading. Continue sharing the book at another time. When you do pick up the book again, be sure to revisit the parts you have already read. Most importantly, enjoy the book!

Be a Vocabulary Detective

You will find a word list on page 5. Words selected for this list are important to the understanding of the topic of this book. Encourage the child to be a word detective and search for the words as you read the book together. Talk about what the words mean and how they are used in the sentence. Do any of these words have more than one meaning? You will find these words defined in a glossary on page 46.

What about Questions?

Use questions to make sure the child understands the information in this book. Here are some suggestions:

> What did this paragraph tell us? What does this picture show? What do you think we'll learn about next? Where do cheetahs live? Could a cheetah live in your backyard? Why/Why not? Other than cheetahs, how many members of the cat family can you name? What do cheetahs eat? What do you think it's like being a cheetah? What if there were no cheetahs? What is your favorite part of the book? Why?

If the child has questions, don't hesitate to respond with questions of your own, such as What do *you* think? Why? What is it that you don't know? If the child can't remember certain facts, turn to the index.

Introducing the Index

The index is an important learning tool. It helps readers get information quickly without searching throughout the whole book. Turn to the index on page 47. Choose an entry such as *fur,* and ask the child to use the index to find out what color a baby cheetah's fur is. Repeat this exercise with as many entries as you like. Ask the child to point out the differences between an index and a glossary. (The index helps readers find information quickly, while the glossary tells readers what words mean.)

Where in the World?

Many plants and animals found in the Early Bird Nature Books series live in parts of the world other than the United States. Encourage the child to find the places mentioned in this book on a world map or globe. Take time to talk about climate, terrain, and how you might live in such places.

All the World in Metric!

Although our monetary system is in metric units (based on multiples of 10), the United States is one of the few countries in the world that does not use the metric system of measurement. Here are some conversion activities you and the child can do using a calculator:

WHEN YOU KNOW:	MULTIPLY BY:	TO FIND:
miles	1.609	kilometers
feet	0.3048	meters
inches	2.54	centimeters
gallons	3.785	liters
tons	0.907	metric tons
pounds	0.454	kilograms

Activities

Make up a story about a cheetah. Be sure to include information from this book. Draw or paint pictures to illustrate your story.

Visit a zoo to see a cheetah. How are cheetahs like other members of the cat family? How are they different? Do you see any cheetah cubs?

Act out being a cheetah. Where do you live? What happens when an enemy is near? How do you get food?

Glossary

coalition: a group of male cheetahs living together

cubs: cheetah babies

den: a quiet, safe place

endangered: only a few of a kind of animal are still living, so the species may die out forever

extinct: no members of a kind of animal are still living

habitat: an area where a kind of animal can live and grow

litter: a group of cheetah cubs born together

mantle: thick, gray fur that grows on the head and back of a baby cheetah

poachers: people who kill animals even though it's against the law

predators (PREH-duh-turz): animals that hunt other animals for food

prey: animals that are hunted and eaten by other animals

savannas: large grasslands

territory: an area that male cheetahs protect from other male cheetahs

Index

Pages listed in **bold** type
refer to photographs.

About the Author

Barbara Keevil Parker has shared her love and knowledge of animals through classroom visits and articles for children's magazines. She enjoys observing animals while hiking at Mount Rainier, in Denali National Park, in the woods of New England, or when sitting on the porch in her backyard. A native of Washington State, she now lives in Rhode Island with her husband, Duane. Barbara is a member of the Society of Children's Book Writers and Illustrators. She is also the author of several children's books.